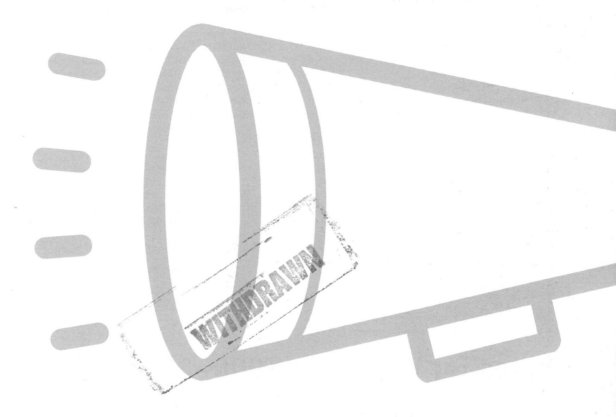

Votes for Women,

c.1900-28

D0320036

 MALCOLM CHANDLER

Heinemann Educational Publishers
Halley Court, Jordan Hill, Oxford, OX2 8EJ
a division of Reed Educational & Professional
Publishing Ltd
Heinemann is a registered trademark of Reed
Educational & Professional Publishing Ltd

OXFORD MELBOURNE AUCKLAND
JOHANNESBURG BLANTYRE GABORONE
IBADAN PORTSMOUTH NH (USA) CHICAGO

© Malcolm Chandler 2001

First published 2001

ISBN 0 435 32731 3
03 02
10 9 8 7 6 5 4 3 2

Designed and typeset by Jonathan Williams
Printed and bound in Spain by Edelvives

Photographic acknowledgements
The author and publisher would like to thank the
following for permission to reproduce photographs:
Bridgeman Art Library: 28A; Hulton Getty/Haines: 13E;
Hulton Getty: 14F, 17H; Imperial War Museum: 30F;
Mary Evans Picture Library/Downey: 6A; Mary Evans
Picture Library/The Fawcett Library: 16G; Mary Evans
Picture Library/The Women's Library: 7B, 11D; Mary
Evans Picture Library: 10A, 23A, 29C; Topham Picture
Source: 21L
Cover photograph: © Hulton Getty
Picture research by Thelma Gilbert

Written sources acknowledgements
The author and publisher gratefully acknowledge the
following publications from which written sources in the
book are drawn. In some sources the wording or
sentence structure has been simplified:

A. Marwick *Women at War, 1914–1918* (Fontana 1977)

M. Pugh *Women's Suffrage in Britain, 1867–1928*
(London Historical Association 1980)

Votes for Women, c.1900–28

Contents

Women and the vote in 1900

Nobody today could possibly imagine that all of the women in Britain, more than half of the population, could be prevented from voting in a general election. Yet that was the case in 1900. In fact, in that year, there was only one country in the world where women were allowed to vote and that was New Zealand. By 1918, when many women in Britain gained the vote for the first time, there had been little change. Only six countries gave women the vote from 1900 to 1917: Australia in 1902, Finland in 1906, Denmark in 1915, Iceland in 1915 and Russia in 1917.

KEY TERMS

Women's suffrage
The right of women to vote in general elections.

Suffragist
A member of the National Union of Women's Suffrage Societies (NUWSS) who campaigned using peaceful methods.

Suffragette
A member of the Women's Social and Political Union (WSPU), a more militant organisation that sometimes used violence to further its aims.

Franchise
The right to vote in political elections.

Progress in the 1890s

In the mid-1890s the tide had seemed to be turning in favour of giving women the vote.

- In 1893 women in New Zealand were allowed to vote for the first time.

- In 1894 a petition for votes for women in Britain gained 250,000 signatures.

- In 1897 the House of Commons voted in favour of votes for women with a majority of 71. The Bill, like all before it, got no further, but it seemed to suggest that the vote for women was achievable in the near future. This appeared to be all the more likely when Arthur Balfour, the Conservative Leader of the House of Commons, and later Prime Minister 1902–05, admitted that the next reform of Parliament would have to include votes for women.

- Women were also beginning to make progress in other fields. They could join the medical profession and could also sit on School Boards and as Guardians of the Poor. A series of Married Women's Property Acts protected them from husbands who were out to steal their belongings after marriage.

But by 1900 all of this progress seemed to be getting nowhere. The problem was that women could only get the vote if it were given to them by men.

What was the situation in 1900?

In 1900 there was a general election in Britain. The main issue in the election was the Boer War in South Africa, which had begun in 1899. The election took place just after a number of besieged towns in South Africa were relieved by British forces. The most famous was Mafeking. The Conservatives, who had been in power since 1895, made the most of the British forces' successes and the election became known as the 'khaki election'.

Approximately 7 million people were entitled to vote in the 1900 general election, out of a total population of some 42 million. Every one of them was a man. Even so, two women did play a small role in the 1900 general election. Mrs Josceline Bagot in South Westmorland and Lady Dickson-Poynder in Wiltshire both wrote and signed the election addresses of their husbands. Both men were serving in South Africa.

But that was as close to voting as women got in 1900. In other ways 1900 was a bad year for women's suffrage.

The 1900 general election

Firstly, the results of the general election were not very encouraging. The chart below shows the result:

Conservative	402
Liberal	184
Irish Nationalist	82
Labour Representation Committee	2

The Conservative Party was almost completely against votes for women and none of the other parties was completely in favour.

The only political party that supported votes for women was the Independent Labour Party, but it was of very little importance.

Secondly, the Women's Suffrage Bill, which was put before Parliament in 1900, was heavily defeated. Similar bills had come before the House of Commons at regular intervals during the late nineteenth century. In fact, by 1914 Parliament had voted almost 50 times on votes for women. In 1900, however, MPs were too busy with events in South Africa to give any real attention to women.

Who could vote in 1900?

In 1900 all voters were men, but not all men could vote. Qualifying for the vote was not a simple matter. Most men gained the vote through the 'household franchise'. This allowed the head of a household to vote, providing he was a man, 21 years of age or over, and had either been a householder for six months or had lived in lodgings for at least twelve months. This meant that many men could not vote, for example if they lived with their parents or did not have a permanent address.

The voting system was not only biased in favour of men, but also in favour of middle-class, wealthy men. This was to be very important in the years from 1900 to 1914. Most proposals for votes for women were based on the idea that women should be entitled to vote on the same terms as men. Many politicians of all parties agreed that in the end women deserved the right to vote, but they were afraid that making changes would favour one party or another. In general, it was thought that giving the vote to women on the same terms as men would help the Conservative Party most, since women were expected to vote Conservative. For this reason the Labour Party began to lose interest in votes for women from 1906.

Women's status as voters in local government

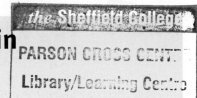
Many of the arguments used against votes for women now seem silly. Women were accused of being too weak to stand up to the strain of politics. Some men said that women would simply vote for the best-looking male candidate. Others said that women would not be able to make up their minds since it took so long for their wives to decide which dress to wear. Many people quoted the Bible or Queen Victoria, who was completely opposed to votes for women. On the other hand, there was plenty of evidence that women were perfectly capable of exercising sensibly the right to vote.

Local councils

Since the 1870s women had been playing a more and more important role in local government in Britain. The 1869 and 1882 Municipal Councils Acts allowed women to vote in council elections. Women could also vote in elections for School Boards from 1870, for Boards of Health from 1875 and in elections to the London County Council from 1889. The Local Government Acts of 1894 and 1899, which set up district and borough councils, also included women as voters.

There was no evidence that women voting did any harm to local democracy, but opponents of women's suffrage were able to stop any further progress. In the first elections for the London County Council, Lady Sandhurst stood and was elected for Brixton. Her opponent objected to her election on the grounds that she was a woman. The Returning Officer who oversaw the election overruled the objection, but the case then went to court. The judge decided that Lady Sandhurst could not take her place. Despite an appeal, the decision stood. This was because, although all of the acts specifically allowed women to vote, none of them stated that women could be elected. It was not until 1907 that a law was passed that allowed women to sit on county councils and borough councils. Nevertheless, by the outbreak of the First World War in August 1914, there were more than 3000 women sitting on councils, local boards and acting as Poor Law Guardians.

This distinction between voting and being a candidate was remembered in 1918. The Representation of the People Act gave women the vote in general elections and the Eligibility of Women Act gave them the right to be elected to Parliament (see page 26).

CASE STUDY

Lady Margaret Sandhurst was a Liberal and stood as a candidate for Brixton in the first elections for the London County Council in 1889. She was elected along with a fellow Liberal, Sir Edmund Verney. She defeated one of her Conservative opponents by over 300 votes and another by over 600 votes. Unfortunately for her, one of her Conservative opponents was the son of

Beresford Hope, a leading opponent of votes for women. He objected to Lady Sandhurst's election on the grounds that she was a woman. When the Returning Officer supported her, he took the case to court. Lady Sandhurst appealed against the decision, but she lost even though the judge who heard the case was a supporter of women's rights.

The growth of the NUWSS and the WSPU

By 1900 the campaign for votes for women had already been in existence for more than 30 years. For much of that time the leading figure in the campaign had been Lydia Becker, who came from Manchester. Many local societies were formed as well as several national organisations, such as the Primrose League and the Women's Liberal Foundation. These societies organised many meetings and presented massive petitions to Parliament. The petition in 1894 was the largest of all.

Millicent Garrett Fawcett and the NUWSS

When Lydia Becker died in 1890, leadership of the movement passed to Millicent Garrett Fawcett. In 1897 the National Union of Women's Suffrage Societies (NUWSS) was formed. This brought together 500 local organisations with more than 50,000 members, many of them men. Millicent Fawcett became the President of the NUWSS and remained so until 1919. However, it was her elder sister, Elizabeth Garrett Anderson, who achieved a notable first for women in politics. She had been the first woman to qualify as a doctor in Britain, and in 1908 she was elected Mayor of Aldeburgh, the first woman to be elected to such a position in Britain.

Under Millicent Fawcett's leadership, the NUWSS used peaceful and legal ways to try to win the vote for women. Its campaign was summed up in its address for telegraphs: 'Voiceless London'. The work of the NUWSS continued throughout the early years of the twentieth century. Some women, however, became dissatisfied with peaceful methods and thought the only way to get votes for women by was by using more aggressive methods. These women formed the Women's

Social and Political Union (WSPU) and became known as 'Suffragettes'. Many 'Suffragists', as members of the NUWSS were called, were not opposed to the methods of the 'Suffragettes', they simply did not believe that they would work. Without the groundwork of the NUWSS, however, the campaign for votes for women would have been much weaker.

SOURCE A

▲ Millicent Garrett Fawcett.

The WSPU

The most important figure in the creation of the WSPU (Women's Social and Political Union) was Dr Richard Pankhurst. He was a firm supporter of votes for women and had stood as a candidate for the Independent Labour Party in the 1895 general election. He was defeated, but continued his campaign until he died suddenly in 1898.

In the 1890s the Pankhursts were living in London. Their house was often used for meetings of the Women's Franchise League. But by the time of her husband's death, Emmeline Pankhurst and her children had moved back to Manchester, where she had been brought up. Manchester had also been the home of Lydia Becker and was a centre of the women's suffrage movement. On her husband's death Emmeline Pankhurst decided to continue his campaign.

Emmeline Pankhurst

Emmeline Pankhurst became involved in the activities of the Labour Party and in 1903 decided to form an organisation for women within the Labour Party. She intended to call it the Women's Labour Representation Committee, but Christabel, her eldest daughter, persuaded her to change the name at the last moment. So, the Women's Social and Political Union was founded at a meeting on 10 October 1903 in Emmeline Pankhurst's house, 62 Nelson Street, in Manchester. The demand of the Union was for 'immediate enfranchisement', or the right to vote.

From 1903 to 1905 the members of the WSPU spoke at many Labour Party meetings in Lancashire. The main speakers were Emmeline Pankhurst and her daughters Christabel and Sylvia, but they soon attracted an important recruit. After a meeting in Oldham, Annie Kenney, a factory worker, came forward and joined the organisation. She became one of the few working-class members of the WSPU.

Women's suffrage bills

The most important sign of the influence of societies like the NUWSS was the number of bills for women's suffrage that came before the House of Commons in the late nineteenth and early twentieth centuries. All of these were Private Members' Bills. These are proposed by MPs and do not have the backing of the government. Usually they have no chance of becoming law, unless the MP introducing the bill gets priority over other issues. But even then it is very easy for either the government or the opposition to prevent the bill becoming law by making sure that there is not enough time for it to be discussed in Parliament. This happened repeatedly. In 1905, for example, a Conservative MP managed to prevent a bill for votes for women being discussed by talking for several hours about whether carts should have a rear light at night.

SOURCE B

▲ **Photographs of the Pankhurst family, from left to right: Sylvia, Christabel, Richard and Emmeline.**

The campaigns for women's suffrage before 1914

Why did the WSPU begin a campaign of disruption in 1905?

One important reason for the WSPU's move to more militant action was the failure to make any progress using peaceful and legal methods. In 1902 women in Australia were given the vote, but when a bill was introduced into the House of Commons it was passed by 182 votes to 68 and then got no further.

A second reason was the debate on 12 May 1905, when a bill for votes for women was talked out by Conservative MPs. Mrs Pankhurst and other members of the WSPU were in the House of Commons for the debate and saw at first hand how MPs could use the Commons procedures to resist the bill. Outside they tried to hold a meeting and their names were taken by the police.

A third reason was Emmeline Pankhurst's growing disappointment with the Labour Party. As the general election approached, Labour leaders began to pay less attention to votes for women. This was partly because they felt that there were much more important issues to concentrate on. Votes for women was not going to win them seats in the election. But there was another issue that was beginning to worry the Labour Party. The WSPU was not calling for all women to get the vote. It was demanding the vote on the same terms as men. Labour leaders believed that this would favour the Conservative Party because women householders would be more likely to vote Conservative.

Christabel Pankhurst, Annie Kenney and Flora Drummond

The change of approach came on 13 October 1905, at a Liberal Party election meeting in the Free Trade Hall in Manchester. This was the first meeting in the campaign by Winston Churchill to win the seat of North West Manchester. Churchill had been a Conservative, but had recently left the party and joined the Liberals. Christabel Pankhurst and Annie Kenney attended the meeting and when questions were invited, Annie stood up and asked Churchill: 'If you are elected, will you do your best to make Women's Suffrage a government measure?' Churchill did not answer the question. Christabel and Annie began to shout: 'The question, the question, answer the question', and were thrown out of the meeting. Outside, they tried to speak to the crowd as it left the hall, but were arrested.

On the following day, 14 October, Christabel was fined 10 shillings, with the alternative of seven days in jail, and Annie was fined 5 shillings, or three days in jail. Both refused to pay. This became a tactic used by all members of the WSPU because it attracted more attention. Winston Churchill attempted to pay the fines at Strangeways Jail, but the governor refused to accept the money. So the first Suffragette martyrs had been created.

The WSPU made the most of the event. When the two girls were released it organised a demonstration in the Free Trade Hall, which attracted great publicity. It also led to a flood of new recruits. The most important was Flora Drummond, who became one of the leaders of the WSPU and was later nicknamed 'The General'.

The 1906 general election

The general election of 1906 was a massive victory for the Liberals and completely changed the make-up of the House of Commons. The chart below shows the results:

Liberal	377
Conservative	157
Irish Nationalist	83
Labour	29
Trade Union	24

The election result gave the Liberals complete control of the House of Commons. Not only did they have an overall majority (more MPs than all the other parties put together), but they could also count on the support of the Irish, Labour and Trade Union MPs. The WSPU expected that the result would lead to an Act of Parliament giving the vote to women.

The WSPU moves to London

In early 1906 the WSPU took an important decision. Until then it had been based in Manchester, but the Pankhursts decided that it was time to move the headquarters to London. It was a brave decision because it would almost certainly lead to greater expense. At first there was just Annie Kenney and Sylvia Pankhurst sharing a room in West London. The two of them decided to organise a meeting at Caxton Hall in Central London on 19 February 1906, the day of the opening of Parliament after the general election. Emmeline Pankhurst came down from Manchester for the meeting.

In one respect the news was bad. The King's Speech, which outlined government policy for the next year, contained nothing about votes for women. Emmeline Pankhurst led a procession from Caxton Hall to the House of Commons to protest. In another way, however, the meeting was extremely fortunate. For the first time Emmeline Pankhurst met Emmeline Pethick-Lawrence and her husband Frederick. The two joined the WSPU and Emmeline Pethick-Lawrence became the treasurer. Her husband had what most other members of the WSPU did not, money and a keen eye for business. For the next six years the Pethick-Lawrences were vitally important members of the WSPU.

The WSPU and the Liberal Party

From early 1906 the WSPU declared war on the Liberal government for failing to do anything about votes for women. In fact, the prime minister, Sir Henry Campbell-Bannermann, was in favour of women's suffrage, but his cabinet was divided. The WSPU knew that Herbert Asquith, the Chancellor of the Exchequer, was against giving women the vote and so he was picked on over and over again. His house in London was picketed and if he spoke at meetings he was interrupted and heckled. Lloyd George, who had voted in favour of women's suffrage on a number of occasions, was also made a target.

Militant action

These actions led to more arrests. In October 1906, eleven Suffragettes, including Sylvia Pankhurst and Emmeline Pethick-Lawrence, were arrested for causing a disturbance outside the House of Commons. Mounted police were used to prevent them reaching Parliament. They were fined £10 each, with an alternative of two months in prison. They all refused to pay and were sent to Holloway Prison. On arrival they were placed in the Second Division – a category of prisoners who were forced to wear prison uniform and were not allowed see friends or write letters. This was another propaganda victory for the WSPU,

Suffragette activities

Over the next two years the League and the WSPU became more and more daring and inventive in their protests. In January, members of the WSPU tried to speak to members of the Cabinet in Downing Street. One woman, Edith New, chained herself to railings outside and shouted 'Votes for Women' until the chains were removed. Flora Drummond, 'The General', ran into 10 Downing Street and was actually forced out by members of the Cabinet.

A few days later, four members of the League attempted to present a petition to King Edward VII while he was travelling in the royal coach. At almost the same time another member dropped thousands of leaflets from a balloon over central London. In February, Emmeline Pankhurst was herself arrested and sent to prison for six weeks. Like all other Suffragettes she refused to promise good behaviour. She served her sentence in solitary confinement and in prison uniform. Emmeline Pankhurst's imprisonment coincided with yet another Private Member's Bill for votes for women. This time it passed its Second Reading by 271 votes to 92, but then got no further.

Suffragette action now became more violent. In June 1908 Edith New returned to Downing Street with Mary Leigh, who later became the first Suffragette to be force fed (see page 13). They adopted a tactic that became one of the Suffragettes' main weapons: stone throwing. They managed to break several of the windows of 10 Downing Street before being arrested.

The Women's Freedom League also became more adventurous. In October 1908 three members chained themselves to the grille in front of the Ladies Gallery in the House of Commons and interrupted the debate by shouting 'Votes for Women'. They were removed, but with the grille still attached.

Events in 1908

In 1908, the NUWSS also became more active. In June it organised a mass demonstration by women in London. This began with a parade of 13,000 women through central London and ended with a meeting at the Royal Albert Hall. Women came dressed as figures from history, including Boadicea and Queen Elizabeth. One group rode all the way from Edinburgh. The Women's Freedom League supported the demonstration, but the WSPU did not. They were preparing their own demonstration in Hyde Park, on 21 June. This started with seven processions from different parts of London, which met at Hyde Park. It attracted a crowd of about half a million people, many of whom, however, had come to enjoy the fun. Emmeline Pethick-Lawrence had spent £1000 advertising the event, which shows how wealthy the movement had become.

Asquith as prime minister

While the campaigns for votes for women seemed to be making progress and gaining more support, hopes of success received a serious blow. In March 1908 Sir Henry Campbell-Bannerman resigned as prime minister and was replaced by Herbert Asquith. Campbell-Bannerman had supported votes for women, but Asquith was known to be an opponent, though his real policy was to 'wait and see'. He said that he was not prepared to introduce change unless he felt that the majority of the people actually wanted it.

The Suffragette response was to renew their attacks on Liberal Cabinet ministers, and on Asquith in particular. At a meeting in Birmingham where Asquith was speaking, two Suffragettes climbed onto the roof of a nearby building and threw slates through the glass roof of the hall. The police tried to dislodge them with fire hoses, but eventually caught them after a chase across the rooftops. Later in the year Asquith was ambushed while he was playing golf, and many of his speeches were interrupted. Lloyd George was also picked on repeatedly. On one occasion a Suffragette managed to lock herself in his car and lecture him until his driver managed to open the door.

▲ Herbert Asquith as Prime Minister.

Organisation of the WSPU

Most of the attacks on Liberal ministers were planned by the WSPU. Volunteers received letters giving details of speakers and places and were asked to go along and cause trouble. The militants usually worked in isolation or in groups of two or three. Other members would not know what was being planned. This made detection much more difficult. By now, thanks to the Pethick-Lawrences, the WSPU was also wealthy enough to be able to pay expenses for hotels and food.

At the same time as the attacks on ministers became more determined, the WSPU kept up pressure at Westminster. It set up a 'Women's Parliament' at Caxton Hall and sent demonstrations to the House of Commons. In June 1909, stone throwing broke many windows in government buildings and more than 100 women were arrested. The Women's Freedom League also continued to put pressure on the government. From July to October 1909 it mounted a picket of the House of Commons in an attempt to give a petition to Herbert Asquith. It failed, but won admiration and respect, and ensured that the League received more favourable treatment from the Liberals than did the WSPU.

Hunger strikes and forced feeding

In 1909 the WSPU introduced a new weapon in its fight against the government. In July, Marion Dunlop-Wallace was sent to Holloway Prison for stamping slogans on the walls of the Houses of Parliament. In prison she refused to eat and was released within a few days. She was the first Suffragette to go on hunger strike. Her action was something that she had decided to do of her own free will and was not part of the tactics of the WSPU. But soon other Suffragettes began copying her, and were also released from prison as a result. In September, the government retaliated. Mary Leigh, who had been sent to prison for throwing slates through the roof where Herbert Asquith was speaking in Birmingham, was force fed through a two-metre-long rubber tube. Meat juice and lime juice cordial were dripped into her stomach through her throat.

Forced feeding became a standard way of treating Suffragettes on hunger strike. Usually the tube was pushed down the throat, but if the victim resisted the tube would be pushed into her stomach through her nose. Hunger strikers were first given a medical inspection

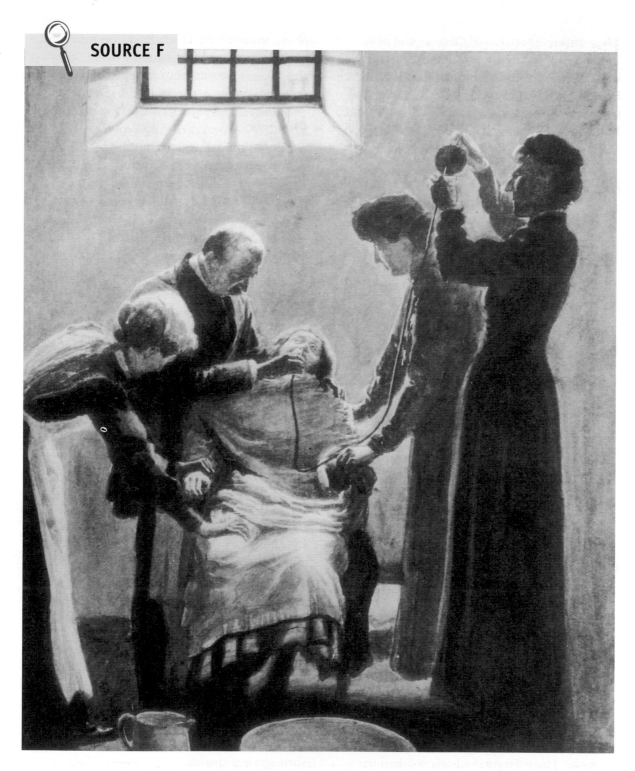

▲ A suffragette poster condemning forced feeding.

by a doctor, to make sure that they were fit enough for this process. But this was often not done very well, as in the case of Constance Lytton, who was force fed in 1910 even though she had a weak heart. The WSPU was able to use forced feeding in its propaganda campaign. Posters showing Suffragettes being held down were very effective, and even King George V suggested that the government should discontinue it.

The Liberal point of view

Looking back it is easy to conclude that the Liberals could simply have given way and granted women the vote. Certainly they could have done so, but by 1909 they had other matters to deal with.

- The Liberals had been elected in 1906 with a massive majority. They had the support of the Labour Party and the Irish Nationalists. The Labour Party was encouraging the Liberals to make changes to the Trade Union law and the Irish Nationalists wanted a Home Rule Bill for Ireland.

- In 1906 the Liberals had begun a series of reforms to tackle the main causes of poverty and ill health in Britain. These had been highlighted in reports published by Charles Booth and Seebohm Rowntree at the beginning of the twentieth century. By 1909 they had passed a series of laws designed to improve the health of children, and an act to provide old age pensions for the first time.

- The Liberals' spending plans meant a rise in taxes which resulted in a clash between the Liberal government in the House of Commons and a massive Conservative majority in the House of Lords. The clash meant that the Liberals faced a possible general election in 1910 and needed to win if they were going to continue their reforms. Since 1906 they had lost by-election after by-election and needed to make sure that they could retain their majority. Votes for women was not a vote winner. Although large crowds turned out to watch suffrage parades, it was estimated that only about 10 per cent of the people were actually in favour of votes for women.

- From 1908 onwards there was a series of major strikes, which continued until 1914. A general strike planned for September 1914 was only called off when the First World War broke out in August 1914.

- In Ireland, plans to grant Home Rule (self-government) led to unrest in Ulster (Northern Ireland) and the creation of two armed forces, the Ulster Volunteers and the Irish Volunteers. In 1914, major violence was only prevented by the outbreak of the First World War.

- In the years leading up to the outbreak of war, there were a number of mass demonstrations in Britain, some to do with trade union disputes, and others caused by anarchists (people who reject government and law and order). On many occasions the government had to order troops onto the streets to deal with the trouble, and more than a dozen protestors were shot by soldiers.

- Finally, the situation in Europe became more and more serious and eventually led to the outbreak of the First World War.

So the Liberals had plenty to think about, quite apart from the Suffragettes. Votes for women appeared to be a minor issue compared with the others that the Liberal government had to deal with.

The Liberals were also faced with the decision about how the vote was to be extended to women. The Liberals wanted to introduce adult manhood suffrage, which meant giving the vote to all men over 21. Some women would also be allowed to vote at the same time, but the WSPU wanted a separate Act of Parliament giving the vote to women. Emmeline Pankhurst actually favoured an extension of the household qualification.

To the WSPU it looked as though the Liberals were simply stalling for time. In fact, the Liberals knew that the great majority of voters in Britain did not regard votes for women as an important issue. They were also aware that an extension of the vote to women as favoured by the WSPU would probably lead to an increase in the number of Conservative voters. In some ways the WSPU did not make the matter any easier. As the tactics of the WSPU became more violent and more personal, Cabinet ministers became more reluctant to give in.

Constance Lytton

The Suffragettes were resourceful, intelligent and determined. Unlike almost all other protest movements of the time, they were mostly middle-class or upper-middle-class women, usually well educated and often well connected. At times this proved very difficult for the Liberals. The case of Lady Constance Lytton is one such example. She was the daughter of Lord Lytton, the Viceroy of India, and took part in demonstrations outside Parliament in 1908. But her real claim to fame came as a result of an incident in October 1909 when she threw a stone at Lloyd George's motor car after he had attended a meeting in Newcastle. Constance Lytton's stone hit the bonnet of the car and she was arrested. In court she refused to pay a fine of £4 and was sent to prison for a month. She immediately went on hunger strike and was released after two days. Instead of being relieved at gaining her freedom, Constance Lytton felt cheated that she had not been able to make the same sacrifice as other Suffragettes. She was determined to make amends.

'Jane Warton'

Two months later, in January 1910, Constance Lytton led a crowd that tried to break into Walton Jail in Liverpool. But this time she was in disguise. She had cut her hair, put on

SOURCE G

▲ Constance Lytton.

spectacles and was wearing cheap, badly fitting clothes. She was again arrested, but in court gave her name as 'Jane Warton'. She was given fourteen days hard labour, but again went on hunger strike. This time she was force fed. After she was released she became paralysed, partly as a result of her treatment.

The WSPU made excellent use of 'Jane Warton' for propaganda, and Constance Lytton posed for photographs in her disguise. The Suffragettes were very skilful in taking advantage of their treatment at the hands of the government and using it to their own advantage. Photographs were taken and published of the leaders in different poses. Emmeline and Christabel appeared in prison clothes looking weak and vulnerable, which they certainly were not! Other photographs showed them formally dressed looking

▲ **Emmeline and Christabel Pankhurst in prison clothes, in a staged photo for propaganda purposes.**

completely respectable. Major events were photographed solemnly, like the funeral of Emily Wilding Davison (see page 21), showing Suffragettes, dressed in white, surrounding the hearse. WSPU posters were equally striking and dramatic. The mouse with a woman in its mouth (see page 21) was one of the most successful. Suffragette propaganda was one of the main reasons why they were able to keep their cause in the public eye for so long.

The WSPU had its own newspaper, *Votes for Women*, to publicise their cause. This reported the demonstrations and gave lists of Suffragette activities. It was edited by Frederick Pethick-Lawrence. When he and his wife left the WSPU in 1912, they took the newspaper with them. To take its place, the WSPU set up a new paper, *The Suffragette*, which was edited by Christabel Pankhurst. This continued to be published until 1920.

Conciliation

Despite the many problems facing the Liberal government, 1910 seemed to offer real chances of votes for women. In January, a general election was held after the House of Lords rejected the Liberal budget of 1909. In 1906, at the last general election, only 48 candidates mentioned women's suffrage in their election addresses. In January 1910, more than 250 candidates included it. Even more important was a speech by Asquith in which he promised that the Liberals would introduce a Parliamentary Reform Bill to which would be added an amendment giving the vote to women.

Both the WSPU and the Women's Freedom League suspended militant action before the general election, but the results were disappointing for the Liberals.

The general elections of 1910

Liberal	275
Conservative	273
Irish Nationalist	82
Labour	40

However, with the support of Labour and the Irish MPs, as the chart shows, the Liberals still had a majority in the Commons.

MPs from all parties joined the 'Conciliation Committee', which then produced the Conciliation Bill. This was a compromise that was intended to give some women the vote. There were only two main clauses in the Bill. The first would give the vote to all women who owned a house, part of a house or just a room. The only condition was that they must have complete control over it. This meant that a husband and wife could not both vote if they lived in the same house. The owners of shops would also be able to vote, providing their premises were worth at least £10 a year in rent. These conditions meant that almost all working women would be left without the vote.

The Conciliation Bill was supported by the WSPU. The Suffragettes were interested in getting the vote for some women. They believed that there was a principle at stake. But the Bill was attacked by Lloyd George and Churchill (Source I), among others. Because they believed that the Bill would play into the hands of the Conservative Party by creating many more Conservative voters. In the end, the Conciliation Bill passed its Second Reading by a majority of 299 votes to 189, but then, like all of the others, got no further. The government refused to make time available for it in the House of Commons.

The crisis between the Commons and the Lords led to a second general election in December 1910. The results were very similar to those of January (see chart below).

Liberal	272
Conservative	272
Irish Nationalist	84
Labour	42

Immediately after the election the Conciliation Committee was reformed and a second Conciliation Bill was produced. This suffered the same fate as the first. It won a majority of 167 in the Commons, but then got no further. But, in a letter to Lord Lytton, the Chairman of the Conciliation Committee and brother of Constance Lytton, Asquith promised to keep the pledge he had made before the January election.

He followed this up in November 1911 with a letter to the People's Suffrage Federation in

SOURCE I

It is an anti-democratic bill. It gives an entirely unfair representation to property, as against persons. What I want to know is how many of the poorest classes will be included? It would be perfectly possible for a woman to have a vote while living in a state of prostitution; if she married and became an honest woman she would lose that vote, but would regain it through divorce.

Winston Churchill attacks the Conciliation Bill in the House of Commons, 12 July 1910.

which he promised that in the next session of Parliament he would introduce a bill in favour of adult suffrage. An amendment would then be introduced giving the vote to women.

The WSPU steps up its action

Asquith's proposal was attacked by the WSPU. Emmeline and Christabel Pankhurst both condemned it as betraying women. The reason for their opposition was that they wanted women to be given the vote on their own, rather than have it tacked onto a bill in favour of men. The result was a new outbreak of violence by the Suffragettes. Only a few days later, the WSPU organised a rally outside the Houses of Parliament, which ended in a fight with the police. Over 200 women were arrested, including Emmeline Pethick-Lawrence. Emily Wilding Davison also invented a new form of militancy in December 1911, when she set light to letterboxes by dropping rags soaked with paraffin into them. But the real campaign began in the New Year.

Oxford Street

On 1 March 1912, at 4 p.m., Suffragettes broke almost every shop window in Piccadilly Circus, Regent Street and Oxford Street. They used hammers which they had concealed in their clothing. At the same time Emmeline Pankhurst threw stones at the windows of 10 Downing Street. More than 200 Suffragettes were arrested. The police then raided the headquarters of the WSPU and arrested Emmeline Pethick-Lawrence. Christabel Pankhurst managed to escape, and fled to France.

But worse was to come. In the summer and autumn of 1912, Asquith was attacked several times by Suffragettes; on other occasions they whipped men who they mistook for him. In July the Theatre Royal Dublin was almost burnt to the ground by Mary Leigh. At the same time, another Suffragette tried to blow up a nearby cinema. She carried gunpowder in her handbag and set light to it when she arrived, but it did not explode.

Dr Almroth Wright

One reason for the increase in Suffragette violence was a letter sent to *The Times* on 27 March 1912 by Dr Almroth Wright, a doctor at St Mary's Hospital in London (Source J).

That would have been quite bad enough, but Dr Wright went on to claim that militancy was a mental illness and that 50 per cent of women went mad in middle age. Understandably, this letter did little to calm the Suffragettes.

SOURCE J

The recruiting field for the militant suffragists is the million of our excess female population – that million which had better long ago have gone to mate with its complement of men beyond the sea. These are sexually embittered women. Peace will return when every woman for whom there is no room in England seeks rest beyond the sea and when the woman who remains in England comes to recognise that she can, without sacrifice of dignity, give a willing subordination to the husband or father, who, when all is said and done, earns and lays up money for her.

The Times, 27 March 1912.

The Franchise and Registration Bill

In the midst of all this mayhem, Asquith introduced the Franchise and Registration Bill in June 1912. It was a sweeping measure that removed most of the remaining qualifications on the right to vote. Asquith, as he had promised, planned to introduce amendments giving the vote to women when the Bill was discussed by the House of Commons.

In fact there were four amendments, all offering different forms of women's suffrage, but in the end they all came to nothing. When the amendments were put forward the Speaker announced that giving women the vote would change the bill so much that it would have to be withdrawn. It met its end in January 1913. Asquith was shocked and tried to get round the problem by offering to provide time for a Private Member's Bill in favour of votes for women.

The WSPU splits

The increased violence during 1912 had important results for the WSPU. Emmeline and Frederick Pethick-Lawrence left the WSPU and began to work on their own for votes for women. They both believed that more violence would achieve nothing. Sylvia Pankhurst also began to drift away from the movement and spent more time working to improve the lives of the poor in the East End of London. This left the WSPU in the hands of Emmeline and Christabel Pankhurst, who now directed the activities of the Suffragettes. Christabel's commands were relayed to London from Paris by Annie Kenney.

The increased Suffragette violence also brought to an end any co-operation between the WSPU and the NUWSS. Millicent Fawcett had often spoken of her admiration for the Suffragettes but had never approved of violence. The wave of firebombs in 1912 and 1913 were too much for her. Now the WSPU became completely isolated and its members followed the instructions of the Pankhursts without question.

Emmeline Pankhurst took no notice of her critics and simply called for more and greater violence. The greens on golf courses were attacked with acid and many had the slogan 'Votes for Women' burnt into them. The orchid house and tea-rooms at Kew Gardens were wrecked and two railway stations, Saunderton and Croxley Green, were burned down. Suffragettes also managed to plant two bombs in a house belonging to Lloyd George and destroyed part of it.

It was during this increased violence that the Private Member's Bill promised by Asquith came before the House of Commons. It passed its First Reading, but at its Second Reading it suffered the same fate as all other such bills and was defeated by 47 votes in May 1913.

SOURCE K

The activities of the militant Suffragettes had now [1913] reached the stage at which nothing was safe from their attacks. Churches were burnt, public buildings and private residences were destroyed, bombs were exploded, the police and individuals were assaulted, meetings broken up, and every imaginable device resorted to. The feeling in the House, caused by the extravagant and lawless action of the militants, hardened the opposition to their demands, with the result that on 6th of May the Private Member's Bill, for which the Government had in the previous session promised facilities, was rejected on the second reading by a majority of 47.

The attitude of many MPs was summed up by the Speaker of the House of Commons writing in 1925.

The 'Cat and Mouse Act'

The government tried to find a way of dealing with the increased violence. One suggestion was for Suffragettes to be deported. Eventually the government decided on the Prisoners (Temporary Discharge) Bill. This allowed the Home Secretary to release Suffragettes who went on hunger strike if their health suffered. They had to agree to certain conditions and could be re-arrested when their health had improved if they did not.

▲ **Suffragette poster criticising the 'Cat and Mouse Act'.**

At first, the 'Cat and Mouse Act', as the new act quickly became known, appeared to solve the problem. But Suffragettes soon began to pretend to be ill in order to get themselves released, just as they had done when they first began to use hunger strikes. Once out of prison they simply went back to their old ways and there was little that the government could do about it. Emmeline Pankhurst took things one stage further and often appeared in public accompanied by a nurse in order to emphasise how she had suffered. She also had photographs taken of herself and her daughters in prison uniform, for propaganda value.

The 1913 Derby

The WSPU also tried to get maximum propaganda value out of a completely unexpected incident that took place on 4 June 1913. Without the knowledge of the WSPU, Emily Wilding Davison ran onto the course during the running of the Derby and stood in front of the King's racehorse, Anmer. She was seriously injured. An emergency operation failed to save her and she died on 8 June 1913.

On 14 June her body was brought to Victoria Station and was then carried to Kings Cross Station in a vast procession of women.

Attacks on property

The Suffragette campaign to destroy property continued during 1913 and 1914. Many houses were destroyed, as well as Oxted Railway Station, Cambridge University Football Pavilion, Yarmouth Pier, the Bath Hotel in Felixstowe and several churches. Suffragettes also began to attack art galleries. A painting in the National Gallery was slashed in June 1913, and two paintings were attacked at Burlington House. But the most spectacular attack was by Mary Richardson on a famous painting called the *Rokeby Venus* on 10 March 1914. She later described how she wandered around the National Gallery for almost half an hour trying to summon up the courage to slash the painting.

This list of damage caused by Suffragettes in the first week of May 1913 was published in the *Morning Post*, a daily newspaper.

SOURCE M

May 3	Ashley Road School, Aberdeen	£400
May 6	St Catherine's Church, Hatcham	£15,000
May 7	Bishop's Park stand, Fulham	£200
May 10	Boot's warehouse, Nottingham	£1600

▲ *Morning Post*, 1913.

Alongside these spectacular events, the WSPU continued with many less dramatic protests, such as distributing leaflets and holding meetings. Cutting telephone lines became a popular and effective action. There was little danger of being caught and the effects could be widespread. On one occasion the Suffragettes were able to almost completely cut off London from the North of England.

This list of incidents was published in the WSPU's newspaper, *The Suffragette*. All the incidents had taken place in the previous week. It shows that, despite all of the militancy, the Suffragettes still held many public meetings to try to convince people to support their aims.

The extension of Sufragette attacks finally convinced many politicians that they could not give in to such tactics. While a majority of MPs supported the right of women to vote, there was a strong feeling that governments should not be seen to submit to what amounted to terrorism. Whether the Suffragettes' actions actually helped or hindered the progress of women's suffrage is, therefore, open to question.

What is certain is that during the final phase of Suffragette activity, from 1912 to 1914, their actions went way beyond what most women thought was acceptable. Many of the more moderate supporters turned against them. The Suffragists, still led by Millicent Fawcett, now regarded them as a liability rather than an asset.

SOURCE N

Violent protests	5
Arson	11
Explosions	1
Window breaking	1
Telephone wire cutting	2
Use of chemicals	3
Meetings	89

▲ *The Suffragette*, 1913.

The outbreak of the First World War and its impact on Suffragette activities

In June 1914 Emmeline Pankhurst led an attempt to break into Buckingham Palace to present a petition to the King. It failed and Emmeline Pankhurst was arrested and carried away by a police inspector. But less than two months later, Emmeline Pankhurst called off the militant campaign. This was her response to the outbreak of war in August 1914. For its part, the government immediately ordered the release of all Suffragettes held in prison (more than 1000).

The Pankhursts took very different paths after 1914. Emmeline's daughter Sylvia, a pacifist, protested against the war and was arrested, but Emmeline urged women everywhere to support the war effort. Both she and Christabel appeared at many recruitment rallies and urged men to volunteer for the army. Emmeline's youngest daughter, Adela, who had at first been involved in the activities of the WSPU, had by 1914 left for Australia, where she campaigned against conscription.

SOURCE A

▲ Emmeline Pankhurst being removed by police from outside Buckingham Palace, June 1914.

chose. Votes for women would only have become law before the First World War if a major political party had been prepared to accept it as a policy.

SOURCE B

It was one thing to sign a petition or join a suffrage society and quite another to vote against one's party. In those pre-war days every voter in the kingdom might have signed a petition for women's enfranchisement and it would still have been possible for Mr Asquith to lie low and say nothing without the slightest fear of weakening his position.

In 1916 Wilma Meikle summed up the difficulties that had been faced in the years to 1914.

Why had women not been given the vote by 1914?

The most important reason why the Liberals were reluctant to give the vote to women was the fact that it was not politically important. Few people in Britain actually regarded women's suffrage as a major issue. The Anti-Suffrage League set up in 1911 soon gained members and was able to present a petition to Parliament with more than 250,000 signatures against votes for women.

As the Liberals lost seats in by-elections from 1907 to 1909 and then had to fight two close elections over the battle with the House of Lords in 1910, their attention was inevitably drawn to other issues. There were of course many attempts to gain women's suffrage during these years, but all of the bills were free votes. That is to say, MPs were allowed by their parties to vote whichever way they

Then there were the different opinions about what votes for women actually meant. Both of the Conciliation Bills tried to extend the household franchise in different ways, but the Franchise and Representation Bill was intended to introduce adult suffrage. The WSPU did not have a clear policy, but Emmeline Pankhurst appeared to have been ready to accept any offer of votes for women, providing it was not tacked onto an act giving men the vote.

The impact of the Suffragettes' activities

The actions of the WSPU probably did more harm than good. Although they aroused public interest in the issue, they failed to win mass support and made the government reluctant to give in. After all, in many ways the Suffragettes were little better than terrorists. Although they claimed that would never cause any physical harm to life and limb, explosion, arson and repeated attacks on individuals suggested otherwise.

The divisions in the movement for women's suffrage certainly did not help their cause. The creation of the Women's Freedom League in 1907 weakened the influence of the WSPU, and after the resignations of the Pethick-Lawrences in 1912 the violence became more extreme. The damage to churches, property and art eventually turned many people against what was a very worthy cause. It also finally alienated Millicent Fawcett, the leader of the NUWSS. After 1912 the two organisations did not co-operate at all.

The impact of the First World War

When war broke out in 1914 most people expected that it would be over by Christmas. Asquith adopted the slogan 'Business as Usual' and appointed Field Marshal Kitchener, the Secretary at War, to run the war. At first women were hardly affected by the war. In 1914 Queen Mary organised a campaign to encourage women to knit socks and scarves for the soldiers and not much else. A group of women, led by Elsie Inglis, volunteered to go to France and work as nurses, but they were turned down by the army.

The situation changed dramatically in May 1915, when the army in France suddenly found itself very short of shells for guns. The Great Shell Shortage showed that the war effort needed to be taken far more seriously. Lloyd George was appointed Minister for Munitions and began immediately to increase the production of weapons and ammunition. In July 1915 the Suffragettes, led by Christabel Pankhurst, organised a Right to Work March in London. Over 30,000 women took part.

Munitions

By the end of 1915 things were very different. 2.5 million men had volunteered for active service. An army of that size needs vast supplies of munitions, and more and more women were needed to help supply them by taking the jobs of the men who had gone to fight. Many women also began to work in the new factories that opened to produce planes, weapons and ammunition. Munitions work could be very dangerous and very unpleasant. Explosive powder could make the skin turn yellow (those women were named 'canaries') and women could catch lung diseases. Safety precautions were basic and some women became unable to have children. But hundreds of thousands of women worked in these factories for high wages, £3 a week. Many women left their jobs as domestic servants for the freedom that the wages in munitions factories gave them.

Opposition to women workers

The employment of women was not always popular. In 1915 there were strikes against women workers when some men complained of dilution – unskilled women taking over the jobs of skilled men. The government was forced to sign agreements with trade unions stating that women would not keep their jobs at the end of the war. The need for women workers became even greater, however, when the Military Service Acts were passed. These introduced 'conscription', or compulsory military service, into Britain for the first time. This meant that even more women were needed to fill men's jobs. By the end of the war 3.5 million men had been conscripted.

Women in the armed forces

Women were also recruited into the armed services for the first time. Women in the First Aid Nursing Yeomanry (FANY) were used as nurses – by 1918 there were about 45,000 – and women in the Voluntary Aid Detachments (VAD) were used as drivers and secretaries. In January 1917 the Women's Auxiliary Army Corps was set up, followed by the Women's Royal Naval Service and the Women's Royal Air Force.

In the countryside women joined the Land Army and took the places of farm-workers. 'Land girls' began to wear trousers, which became acceptable. But there were only about 13,000 women altogether in the Land Army.

Women in industry

Another industry that gained many women recruits was the motor car industry, where women began to work as mechanics or drivers. The motor car industry developed a great deal during the war as the army realised how useful motor cars, lorries and tanks could be. Women also found work in the aeroplane industry. Elsewhere in the economy, women also took over many clerical jobs in banks and began to work as postal workers and on buses as conductresses.

How did the war change the role and status of women in Britain?

Although many women found themselves earning good wages for the first time during the war, they were always paid less than men, and were not promoted as often as their male colleagues. Also, they were often given the most dangerous jobs to do. In addition, male workers played practical jokes on them, and in 1915, there were strikes against the use of women workers. Actions like these meant that when the war ended most women were sacked and their jobs were given back to men. There was also a big campaign to persuade women to give up their jobs and go back to being housewives. Women who refused to give up their jobs were sometimes attacked. The phrase 'Heroines to Scroungers' was used to describe them.

But the war did lead to real changes in social attitudes. Women had more freedom after the war. Their clothing became much simpler, with shorter skirts and sleeves. Hairstyles changed and it became acceptable for women to wear trousers.

The Representation of the People Act, 1918

The work of women in the war effort on its own might not have been enough to win the vote. A key factor in getting women the vote was the attempt by the government to produce a new electoral register in 1916. It soon became obvious that many of the men who had been entitled to vote in 1914 had now lost the vote. This was because they were in the army, which meant that they no longer qualified under the household franchise. The government therefore decided it would be easier to give the vote to all men over the age of 21. This was done in the Representation of the People Act of 1918.

The government's decision was also influenced by the fact that many men had spent a long time in the armed forces and that many had been conscripted. It seemed unfair for a man to fight for his country, but at the same time have no say in how the country was governed. The government's concern was shown by a temporary clause in the Act which extended the vote to men over the age of eighteen who had served in the war.

The Representation of the People Act gave the government the opportunity to give the vote to women at the same time. Before 1914 the government had not wanted to appear to be giving in to women, but now it could allow women the vote without any such fear. There was just one other concern, however. Emmeline Pankhurst had called off Suffragette actions in August 1914, but there was nothing to stop them starting again when the war was over. Christabel Pankhurst was still editing the WSPU newspaper, The Suffragette, and she could easily have called for renewed action. There may or may not have been a serious threat, but it was one that was better avoided.

By 1918 there were in fact few politicians who were prepared to argue against women's suffrage. Women had played a vital and responsible role on the Home Front during the war and most of the old arguments against women's suffrage were no longer valid. Herbert Asquith, who had opposed votes for women before 1914, now spoke out in favour. He even admitted that the war could not have been won without the efforts of women. When the vote was finally taken in the House of Commons in December 1917, there were 364 votes in favour and 23 against.

Votes for women

The Act did, however, have a sting in its tail. Although men were given the vote at the age of 21, women were not. Not only did they have to wait until they were 30 to vote, but they also had to be householders or married to a householder. So the household franchise survived. The main reason for this was that Parliament did not want women voters to outnumber men. There was also the belief that women were not as mature as men and therefore needed to be older and show more responsibility before they could be trusted with the vote. Altogether, 6 million out of 13 million women gained the vote in 1918.

The government nearly failed to put a clause into the Act which allowed women to become MPs. This had been a problem with all of the late nineteenth- and twentieth-century local government acts. At the last minute, in November 1918, just before the general election in December, the government rushed the Eligibility of Women Act through Parliament. This allowed women to stand as candidates. In the event only one woman was elected, Countess Markiewicz, who was elected for Sinn Fein in South Dublin. Sixteen other women stood for Parliament and all were defeated. They included Christabel Pankhurst and Emmeline Pethick-Lawrence.

Legal changes

Equally important were the legal changes made at that time. In 1919 the Sex Disqualification Act made discrimination against women in some professions illegal. However, it did not have much effect. In 1922 the Law of Property Act gave husbands and wives equal rights to inherit each other's property. In 1923 divorce became easier for women: they could now divorce their husbands on equal terms. Until 1923 a wife had to prove two causes for divorce out of adultery, cruelty and desertion, while a man had only to prove one.

Women also gained more control over their lives in the 1920s because contraception became available for the first time, through the work of Marie Stopes, who founded the first birth-control clinic in London in 1921. Few women were able to take advantage of this at first, but then the social stigma of using contraception began to decrease.

The professions

After the war, several professions began to accept more women. The vast number of casualties during the First World War had meant that more women doctors were needed. The legal profession also began to accept women. It also became commonplace to see women working as teachers in elementary (primary) schools.

The Representation of the People Act, 1928

Legal and social changes soon made the restrictions on the voting rights of women look pointless. In addition, the general elections of the 1920s were no different from those of the pre-war period. Giving women the vote had not been the disaster that some had predicted. Politics continued to be dominated by men and by 1928 there were only four women MPs in the House of Commons. In any case, the Act of 1918 had been regarded as a 'trial run' by many people and it was soon clear that it had been successful. In 1928, therefore, a further Representation of the People Act gave women the vote on the same terms as men.

In 1900 all women had been excluded from national politics. By 1928, although politics was still dominated by men, women could

now vote and participate at all levels. Of the major figures involved in the struggle for votes for women, Emmeline Pankhurst died in 1928, just days after women were given the vote at 21. By then her days as a militant had long passed and in 1926 she had joined the Conservative Party. Frederick Pethick-Lawrence had become an MP and had spoken out strongly in favour of the 1928 Act. Christabel Pankhurst became deeply religious and gave lectures on the second coming of Jesus Christ. Her younger sister Sylvia, who had left the WSPU in 1913, became heavily involved in Socialism. Whether the efforts of the WSPU and other organisations helped or hindered the eventual attainment of women's suffrage, or whether it was the result of other events, is for you, as a historian, to judge.

Sample coursework assignment

SOURCE A

What a Woman may be, and yet not have the Vote

MAYOR　NURSE　MOTHER　DOCTOR or TEACHER　FACTORY HAND

What a Man may have been, & yet not lose the Vote

CONVICT　LUNATIC　Proprietor of white Slaves　Unfit for Service　DRUNKARD

▲ Suffragette poster produced in 1912.

SOURCE B

'Votes for women' is the shrill cry of a number of discontented ladies. But the truth is that Women were and are destined to make voters rather than to be voters themselves. It cannot be denied that women suffer great injustice at the hands of men. But this is the result of the way in which mothers have reared their sons and still continue to rear them.

From a book written in 1907 called *Woman or Suffragette* by Marie Corelli.

▲ Cartoon drawn by Bernard Partridge in 1906. The two women are both campaigners for female suffrage, but the one on the left is a Suffragist; the one on the right is a Suffragette. The caption reads: 'THE SHRIEKING SISTER'. The person on the left, described as the sensible woman, says: 'YOU help our cause? Why, you're its worst enemy!'

SOURCE D

What good did all this violent campaigning do us? We have often been asked that question. For one thing our campaign made women's suffrage a matter of news – it had never been that before. Now the newspapers are full of us.

The argument of politicians and the Suffragists has always been that once public opinion swings our way then without any force at all women will be given the vote. We agree that the public must be educated, but in 1906 there was a very large section of the public who were in favour of women's suffrage. But what good did that do the cause? We called upon the government to give us the vote but they didn't. So, now we will fight for our cause.

Part of a book called *My Own Story* by Emmeline Pankhurst, one of the leading Suffragettes. It was written in 1912.

SOURCE E

I have no hesitation in voting against the principle of giving the vote to women. In giving women the right to vote we will ultimately put the control of the government of this country into female hands.

Part of a speech given by a Member of Parliament in 1913.

SOURCE F

ON HER THEIR LIVES DEPEND

WOMEN MUNITION WORKERS

Enrol at once

▲ **Poster produced by the government in 1916.**

SOURCE G

	July 1914	July 1918
Metal industries	170,000	594,000
Chemical industries	40,000	104,000
Government offices	2,000	225,000
Food, drink and tobacco	196,000	235,000

▲ **Women in employment in Britain. Statistics from a school textbook, published in the 1980s.**

SOURCE H

A very simplified view would see the vote as a reward for loyal wartime service. However, careful study shows how little change resulted from the war, not how much.

In the newspaper reports of the time women workers received a warm welcome; but in farms, hospitals and factories they were greatly resented. This reflects most men's attitudes towards women at the time. Men felt happiest if women became nurses, providers of refreshments for the troops and brought up the fighting men of the future. Politicians themselves agreed with the idea that the woman who had brought children up successfully had performed a service for the government which could be rewarded by giving the vote to such loyal citizens.

The age limit of 30 for women was agreed by politicians because these women seemed to be more sensible and more likely to vote the same way as their husbands.

From a history book called *Women's Suffrage in Britain, 1867–1928*, written in 1980.

SOURCE I

To say that the war brought votes for women is to make a very rough generalisation, yet one which contains some truth. The question of women's rights must not be isolated from other great social and political changes that were happening as a result of the war. During the four years of conflict a tremendous mood favourable to change had been created.

From a history book called *Women at War, 1914–1918*, written in 1977.

SOURCE J

My opposition to women's right to vote is well known. However, for three years now the Suffragettes have not restarted that horrible campaign of violence. Not only that, they have contributed to every service during this war except that of fighting. I therefore believe that some measure of women's suffrage should be given.

Part of a speech by Herbert Asquith in the House of Commons in 1917. Asquith had been Prime Minister from 1908 to 1916 when he had opposed giving women the vote.

? Assignment One: Objective 1

1. Why did a campaign for women's suffrage develop in the years after 1870? (15)

2. Describe the ways in which the methods of the Suffragists and Suffragettes were different. (15)

3. Women over 30 gained the vote in 1918 mainly because of women's contribution to the war effort. Do you agree? Explain your answer. (20)

(Total: 50 marks)

? Assignment Two: Objectives 2 and 3

1. Study Source A. What can you learn from Source A about the reasons given by the Suffragettes for demanding votes for women? (6)

2. Study Sources B and C. Does Source B support the evidence of Source C about the Suffragette campaign? Explain your answer. (8)

3. Study Sources D and E and use your own knowledge. Why, despite the Suffragette activity, had women not gained the vote by the outbreak of the First World War? (12)

4. Study Sources F and G. How useful are these two sources as evidence for the contribution of women to the war effort in the years 1914-18? (10)

5. Study Sources H, I and J and use your own knowledge.

   'It was the work that women did during the war that earned them the vote'.

   Use the sources, and your own knowledge, to explain whether you agree with this interpretation. (14)

(Total: 50 marks)